# NO BIGGER THAN MY TEDDY BEAR

# NO BIGGER THAN

# MY TEDDY BEAR

## Valerie Pankow

### illustrations by Gwen Connelly

Family Books                    Petaluma, California

Library of Congress Cataloging-in-Publication Data
Pankow, Valerie
No bigger than my teddy bear.
Summary: A little boy describes how the hospital staff
provided care for his premature baby brother.
1. Infants (Premature)—Hospital care—Juvenile literature.
2. Neonatal intensive care—Juvenile literature.
[1. Babies—Hospital care.  2. Neonatal intesnsive care.]
I. Connelly, Gwen, III. II. Title RJ250.P36  1987  618.92'01  87-17509

ISBN: 978-0-9728460-0-4
Printed in the United States

CPSIA Compliance Information: Batch #0511. For further information contact
RJ Communications, NY, NY, 1-800-621-2556

NO BIGGER THAN
MY TEDDY BEAR

Hi! My name is Dustin.

This is a picture of me with my family.

I have a new baby brother named Brendan.

He's so tiny and small. I think my teddy bear is bigger than he is.

Brendan is a very special baby because he was premature.  That means he was born too soon.  I think he was in a hurry to see me.

This is the hospital where Brendan was born.  He had to stay there a long time because premature babies are tiny and not ready to come home.

When Brendan was in the hospital, he was in a special room called the Intensive Care Nursery. It was a busy room with lots of special machines and lots of very tiny babies no bigger than teddy bears.

One day, I finally got to go see my baby brother in the hospital. First I had to see a nurse, who took my temperature and made sure that I was healthy. I didn't want to give my baby the chicken pox, an earache or even a sore throat. I knew that wouldn't be good for my baby.

Then I washed my hands with special soap, just like the doctors did. I always liked to make lots and lots of bubbles, so I could get my hands very clean.

The first time I got to go into the nursery, I was scared. There were
so many machines, lights, wires, and tubes. There were doctors and
nurses everywhere. But when I saw my baby, I smiled because he
was my new brother.

All of the babies were in special beds. Some were in flat open beds with lights over them to keep them warm. Other babies were in isolettes, which are like plastic boxes you can see through. After the babies were born, they would each get a hat. Each hat was different. Some were blue. Some were yellow. Some were striped, but they were all warm and fuzzy.

Brendan was in an isolette. Mom said the isolette kept Brendan nice and warm all the time. Premature babies are too tiny to keep themselves warm, so the isolette warms them up like a piece of toast.

Sometimes I drew special pictures for Brendan. Mom put them on his isolette so he could see them. That way, Brendan knew I loved him, even if I couldn't be with him.

Mom showed me the leads attached to Brendan's chest. All the babies had them. They looked like big sticker dots with wires coming out of them. The wires were hooked up to a machine called a monitor, which showed the doctors and nurses how fast or slow the baby's heart was beating and how he was breathing.

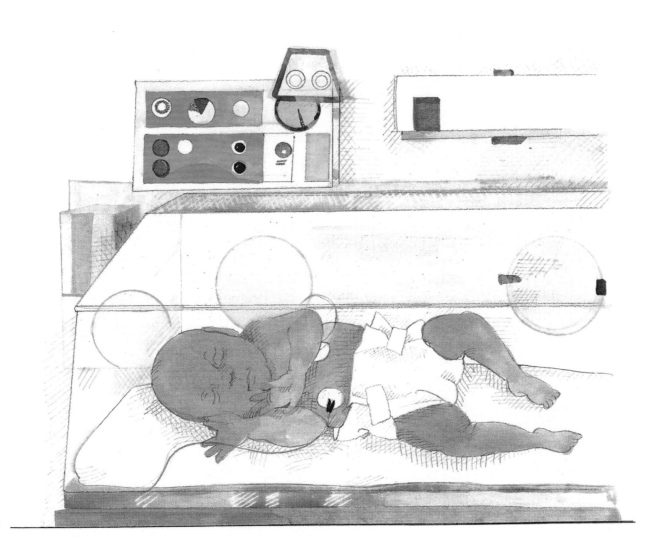

Sometimes, the monitor's alarm would go off. That was a loud scary sound, like a siren. It told the nurses that the baby wasn't breathing fast enough. Then the nurses would help the baby right away.

Once when I was visiting Brendan in the hospital, the phone in the nursery rang. It made such a loud sound that it scared Brendan and his monitor alarm went off. After the nurse patted him on the back and told him it was okay, the alarm stopped beeping. I thought it was pretty funny that my baby was afraid of the phone ringing.

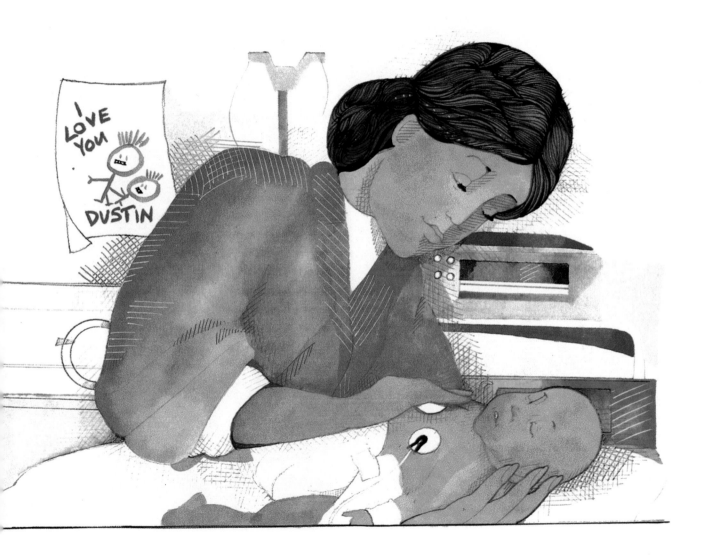

Every day Mom had to go visit Brendan in the hospital. She held Brendan and fed him. Sometimes this made me mad, because I missed my mom. I wished that I could go, too.

When my mom came home from the hospital, we would spend special time together. Then I was happy. We talked about my baby, and we talked about me. Sometimes we read stories, and sometimes we just snuggled.

I really love my mom.

Some days, while my mom and dad were at the hospital, I would play doctor with my teddy bear. My teddy bear would be a premature baby in the nursery. I would put stickers on him and pretend he was in an isolette.

Things were always different when I went to visit my brother. Sometimes there were new babies and new machines. One time when I went there, I couldn't even find my baby. I thought he was lost. But I found him. The nurses had moved around all of the babies and their beds.

Another time when I went to visit Brendan, he had a funny hood over his head. I could hardly see his face. I called it his space helmet. Dad called it his oxygen hood. Dad said it helped Brendan breathe better.

Some of the babies had tubes in their mouths and noses to help them breathe. After a while, many of the babies could breathe by themselves.

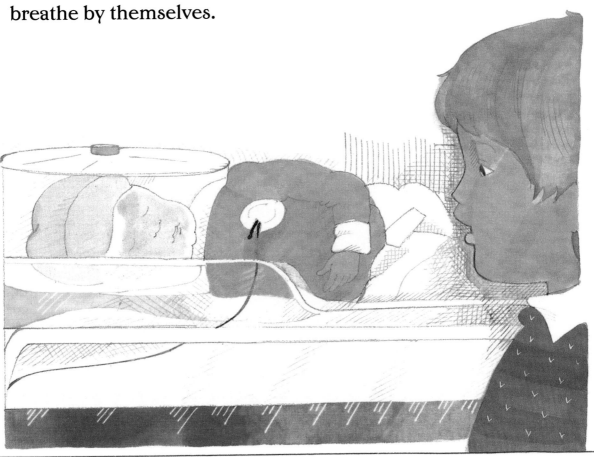

It was fun to see my baby get weighed.  Every day they weighed him to see how much he'd grown.  I liked it when Brendan grew a lot.  Then I knew he was getting better and would be able to come home soon.

Brendan had lots of different nurses.  They would always talk to me and answer my questions.  Sometimes they could even make me smile when I was mad.

This is me holding my tiny baby brother.  He's all bundled up to keep warm.  The nurses would wrap him up in two blankets and put on his warm fuzzy hat.

Then they would give him to me to hold.  I loved to hold my baby and talk to him.

I had to wait a long time before I could help feed my baby. At first, Brendan didn't know how to suck or swallow, so the nurses had to feed him through a tube. I don't think he liked that, but it helped to make him stronger.

As Brendan got bigger and stronger, he began to suck from a small bottle with a soft red nipple. Sometimes he'd suck from Mom's breast. When Mom nursed Brendan, she would hold him in her arms and cuddle him. I know my baby liked that.

Once a nurse gave me a plastic bottle with a soft red nipple, just like Brendan's, for my teddy bear. You know, those babies are no bigger than my teddy bear. My teddy bear likes to be cuddled and fed just like Brendan.

One day, when Mom came home from the hospital, she was very happy. She had a giant smile on her face. She said Brendan was growing and getting so strong that he could come home in a few days.

This is my favorite picture. We're in the nursery getting Brendan dressed. He's finally coming home. But he's still…

NO BIGGER THAN MY TEDDY BEAR!!!